D1345794

Detox

Detox

100 natural ways to cleanse and purify

Carol Morley & Liz Wilde

MQP

MQ Publications Ltd

introduction

The world today is toxic. Food is sprayed with pesticides, air is filled with pollution and our minds are seriously stressed. If you feel tired and run-down, chances are you're suffering from toxic overload and you need to give your body a break to restore balance. Spring cleaning your mind and body will benefit every inch of you. Expect clearer skin, sparkly eyes, improved skin tone and reduced cellulite, a flatter stomach and much more energy. You can't shut out external poisons such as car fumes, smoke, sunlight and office technology, but you can build a strong immune system to cope with the chemical ambush. This little book tells you how. Use it every time you need a pick-me-up.

contents

chapter 1

Spring clean

1 Detoxing simply means dejunking your body. With all the toxic waste we pick up from convenience foods and polluted air, our bodies can't push the poison out fast enough. Which leaves us feeling tired, sluggish and in need of a boost, but give your body a break and you'll feel an instant lift. Other benefits to expect include clearer skin, tighter muscle tone (wave goodbye to your cellulite), a flatter stomach and much more energy. Not bad for a few days' work.

If you're going to follow a detox eating plan, here's what you should avoid:

- *Red meat*
- *Dairy products (butter, cheese, milk and eggs)*
- *Salt*
- *Bread and pastry*
- *Sugar*
- *Cakes and biscuits*
- *Flour and wheat*
- *Sweets and chocolate*
- *Convenience foods*
- *Tea and coffee*
- *Alcohol*
- *Anything containing artificial additives (preservatives, colouring, flavouring etc).*

OK, so it's a long list, but we're only talking two days at a time max. Go on, you know it makes sense.

2 **Plan your detox around a quiet, anti-social weekend.** Not one when you'll have to spend every night watching your friends knocking back the wine while tucking into a massive meal.

3 **All sounds like too much hard work?** Even two days without caffeine, alcohol, sugar and processed food will give your natural elimination process a kick start and leave you feeling fantastic.

11

4 Be brave and give your body a real chance to repair by following a short fast. We're not talking intensive regime here. Health spas may advocate you exist on liquids for a week (and make you pay for the pleasure), but fasting in your own front room should be a more relaxing experience. The idea of fasting is to rest your body so it can clean itself out, not give it a fright. Sudden changes will just leave you feeling sick and dizzy, so begin by eating simple food for a few days before the serious stuff starts. Then decide which of the following foods you fancy fasting on (they all have great health-promoting benefits):

- *Fruit and vegetables (raw or cooked any healthy way you want)*
- *Raw food*
- *Fruit and vegetable juices*
- *Fruit (apples are full of vitamins, minerals and a fibre called pectin which helps flush out toxins)*
- *Grains (brown rice is the most cleansing).*

5 Whatever you choose, drink lots of water and don't exceed two days without supervision or advice from an expert. Lastly, forget fasting if you suffer from heart disease, low blood sugar levels, liver or kidney problems, or you're on any medication, are pregnant, epileptic, anaemic or suffering a serious illness.

6 **Drinking enough water is the best way to keep your body pumping out what's not needed.** Aim to drink at least eight glasses a day during any detox time, as this will speed up the rate toxins leave your body and help fill up your tummy. Check your urine to ensure a healthy fluid intake. Pale yellow is perfect, but any darker means you're not drinking enough.

7 Saying goodbye to toxins can be tough on your body. Temporary side effects may include headaches and other aches and pains, spots, low energy, diarrhoea and even dizziness. Don't panic as these are all signs that your fast is working (and you needed it), but do your body a favour and take it easy. There's never been a better excuse to be lazy.

8 Don't go cold turkey. If you're planning any type of fast, gradually cut down on caffeine, alcohol and processed foods a few days before. Then the day after your good deed, avoid the temptation to return to all your bad ways the minute your alarm goes off. The idea is to learn a few new good habits, not undo all your hard work.

9 You don't need sugar in your tea or coffee. Instead, satisfy a sweet tooth with a teaspoon of more-healthy honey.

10 **During your detox, take a good multivitamin supplement and a vitamin B complex** to give your body the nutrients it needs.

11 **Speed up your detox with a little help from a diuretic essential oil.** Mix a few drops of Fennel, Juniper or Geranium in a tablespoon of vegetable oil and rub onto the soles of your feet (bang in the middle) to stimulate the pressure point relating to your kidneys. Just don't stray too far from a toilet!

17

12 **The simplest way to spring clean your body is with a fruit and veg fast.** Stock up and store in the fridge to retain those all-important nutrients. Then chop, slice, juice, steam or poach – just make sure everything you put in your mouth is fresh. And keep your body's blood sugar level constant by eating or drinking something every two to three hours.

13 **How often do you actually taste your food?** Most meals are eaten far too quickly to taste every flavour, which also has your digestion working overtime to cope with the sudden excitement. By chewing each mouthful slowly, everything will not only taste better, it'll digest better too. And your appetite is better satisfied.

14 **Then again, there's not much to taste if you cook the life out of your food.** Stop boiling your vegetables until they're soggy. Swap your cooking techniques and you'll get more flavour from your food, not to mention more nutrients. Grill, steam or stir-fry for more healthy mealtimes.

15 Fresh juices contain concentrated goodness, and suit a body suffering from over-indulgence as they put minimal strain on your system (they only take 10–15 minutes to digest). Pre-packed juice may contain sugar, colour, flavours and preservatives, so invest in a juicer and make your own. There are so many combina-tions, you need never drink the same juice twice, but avoid too much acidity by mixing fruit and veg in your recipes. Either replace one meal a day, or once a month have a one day juice fast. And drink your juice moments after whizzing as it loses precious vita-mins and minerals fast.

Warning: Don't do the juice thing just before a big date as it may make your breath smell due to toxins being eliminated from your lungs.

Juice ingredients that are tough on toxins:
- *Cabbage* – a great cure for constipation.
- *Parsley* – super potent so mix with other juices.
- *Spinach* – speeds digestion to cleanse, and also clears constipation.
- *Celery* – clears clogged up waste.
- *Beetroot* – a good cleanser for liver, kidney and gall bladder.

LEMON

16 Can't face the thought of a fast? Then try this mini one for size. Eat your last meal before 6pm and then eat a breakfast of fresh fruit the next morning at nine. This gives your overloaded body a full 15 hours to recover. What will it be doing? Processing all the residual foods left hanging around to clog you up.

17 Start each day feeling fresh. Drink a glass of hot water mixed with the juice of half a lemon to cleanse your system, aid digestion and flush out toxins. If the sharp taste sets your teeth on edge, add a small spoonful of honey.

18 If your idea of willpower is not eating the whole bar of chocolate, clear your fridge of tempting treats until your detox is over.

19 **Most of us are only using half our breathing potential,** which means we're not only taking in less oxygen, we're not getting rid of excess carbon dioxide either. Breathing right can help clean out your system, so check your technique. Lie on the floor, place your hands over your stomach and (hopefully) feel it rise when you breathe in and fall when you breathe out. Not so much as a ripple? Practise slowly breathing in and seeing your stomach swell, then slowly breathing out as your stomach shrinks.

20 **Experts say that raw food provides you with a heady cocktail of essential vitamins, minerals and antioxidants** to make you feel your best ever. Fans claim that a raw food diet can cure digestion problems, improve memory and send energy levels soaring.

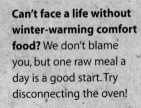

Can't face a life without winter-warming comfort food? We don't blame you, but one raw meal a day is a good start. Try disconnecting the oven!

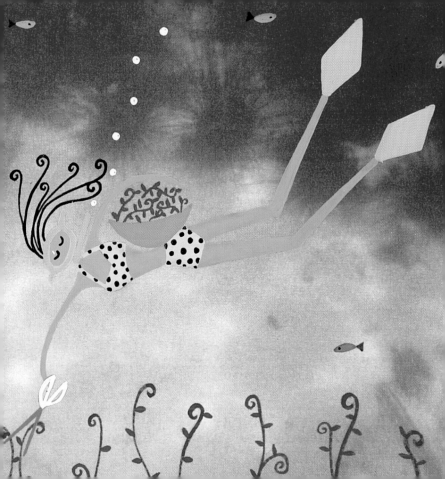

chapter 2

Toxin-free foods

21 **Cut down on toxins entering your body by switching to food that doesn't contain them.** Remember, the further down the food chain you go, the more chances there'll be toxins hiding in your dinner. Eat as much raw, organic food when you can (organic prices are coming down and are sure to drop further). Not only will your average organic apple taste better and crunch louder, it'll also be packed with twice the goodness and none of the badness. Need more convincing? An ordinary innocent apple may have been sprayed with pesticides up to eleven times before it arrives in your supermarket basket. Bet that spoils your appetite.

22 **Popular as an extra health shot in juice bars, wheatgrass is your body's best friend.** This plant essence is seven times richer in vitamin C than oranges, and five times richer in iron than spinach. Add to that its powers to purify your system, enabling the body to absorb nutrients and eliminate toxins, and you've got one powerful detox tool.

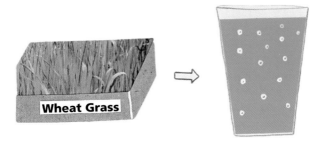

23 **A fast-acting natural diuretic**, cucumber makes for the perfect internal shower.

24 **You can live without food for a while, but only a few days without water is enough to kill you.** The body is made up of around 65% water. This level needs constant topping up or you'll feel tired, suffer poor skin, high cholesterol levels, possible urinary-tract infections (think cystitis) and bowel problems. Drink it, spritz it on your face and eat fruits with a high water content (grapes, plums, pineapple).

25 Water's good for you, right?

Yes, but some are better for you than others. Distilled is the purest choice as it's been heated to boiling point so impurities are separated from the water which becomes steam. This is then condensed back into pure liquid form, while the impurities remain in the residue. Not so pure is your average glass of tap water which in cities may have passed through six to ten pairs of kidneys before yours, meaning you're drinking any number of nasties picked up along the way. Bottled water lands as rain and collects in underground pools, but some experts believe many varieties of bottled water contain minerals that cannot be absorbed by your body. To ensure best regulations, look for bottles labelled 'natural' as these will have come from a protected source with more stringent testing.

26 **The Japanese swear by seaweed, and so should we.**
Seaweed contains alginic acid which bind to harmful waste in your body to aid elimination, and experts also believe it protects against heart disease and boosts the immune system. Shop for dried seaweed in health food stores or Japanese food suppliers.

27 **Don't drench salad in a shop-bought dressing.**
Make your own from virgin olive oil mixed with fresh herbs for a taste that tops any mass produced product.

34

28 **An apple a day really can keep the doctor away.** The humble apple is our richest fruit source of vitamin E, and also contains powerful anti-oxidant vitamins A and C. Add to that minerals such as potassium, magnesium and calcium plus essential amino acids, and you can see why apples are a favourite fasting food. Another reason why apples are perfect for detoxing is down to a fibre called pectin which works at eliminating the

29 Bad snacks:

- *Biscuits*
- *Crisps*
- *Sweets*
- *Salted nuts.*

Good snacks:

- *Dried fruit*
- *Unsalted nuts and seeds*
- *Rice cakes*
- *Raw fruit and veg.*

heavy metals we pick up from pollution. No chance to brush your teeth? Eat an apple and your natural mouthwash, saliva, will be stimulated to clear away the clutter. Wash apples well or buy organic to cut down on possible pesticide residue.

Ok, so it sounds boring, but try it and feel the energy still flowing through your body hours later, rather than the usual brief high followed by a deep-down low.

Teas to drink while detoxing:

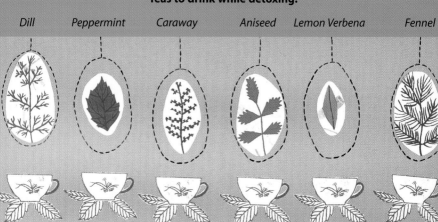

Dill   Peppermint   Caraway   Aniseed   Lemon Verbena   Fennel

30 Who needs a coffee fix?

Herbal teas don't just quench your thirst, they can lift you up, send you to sleep, settle your stomach and much more. Tried one kind and didn't like it? No problem. With so many different combinations of herbs, fruits and flowers to choose from, there's a tea out there for everyone.

31 Other therapeutic teas to choose from:

Camomile – calming and soothing. Drink before bedtime to induce sleep, or after a rich meal to relax a full tummy.

Dandelion – helps flush out excess fluids in your body.

Elderflower – acts as a diuretic to cleanse out your body, and is good to drink for a cold or flu, to ease sore throats and encourage your body to sweat out germs.

Ginger – warms your body on cold days by boosting blood circulation, and is also a good stomach settler when you're feeling sick.

Passionflower – an instant soother after a stressed day, drink before bedtime to help you relax and nod off.

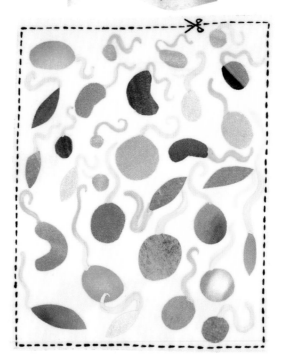

mixed Sprouts

32 Sprouted beans and seeds are crammed with nutritional goodness (raw protein, vitamins and minerals) that's easy to digest. To sprout them, you need to soak beans and seeds in water for up to 15 hours, then pour off the excess and cover. Your seeds will fully sprout in a few days and beans can take up to five. Buy bags of chickpeas, lentils, mung beans, pumpkin seeds and sunflower seeds in the super-market. Or take the short cut and look for ready-sprouted beans and seeds in your local health food shop. Sprinkle on salads and sandwiches, or save them for between meal snacks.

33 Asparagus may be one of the more expensive items in the vegetable aisle, but read on and you may feel like splashing out once in a while. Each spear contains ingredients that relieve indigestion, eliminate water retention and even help stop insomnia. If your budget won't stretch, try celery instead which also helps reduce water retention and sends you off to sleep.

34 **Heard the one about five servings of vegetables a day?** Well, make a couple of those raw and you'll be doing your body even more favours by fighting off everyday infections.

35 **Buy your yogurt live** and it'll contain *lactobacillus acidophilous* and *bifidobacteria*, serious-sounding names of friendly intestinal bacteria that protect your delicate balance within. And choose sheep or goat's milk yogurt as these are easier to digest than cow's.

36 **The right kind of fat is good for you.** Like Omega-3, found in kippers, sardines, salmon and mackerel. Nutritionists know it reduces the risk of cancer and heart disease, not to mention making your skin glow.

37 **Brown rice is the ultimate in waste disposal.** It works by absorbing the litter in your intestine and then flushing it out again. Choose short grain varieties as these have a larger surface area for clutter to cling onto.

38 **Linseed is a bulking agent that assists the passage of waste through your system.** Sprinkle some on your morning fruit or cereal for the healthiest colon in town.

39 **Over-indulged again?** Then be kind to your internal organs by feeding them their favourite foods.

Liver-Friendly Foods:
- *Garlic (fresh or a capsule)*
- *Carrot juice*
- *Red grapes*
- *Beetroot juice*
- *Dandelion tea.*

Kidney-Friendly Foods:
- *Cranberry juice*
- *Melon*
- *Honey in hot water.*

Linseed

40 **Forget fighting off vampires.** Take an (odourless) garlic tablet a day and you need never catch a cold again. This super supplement fights off germs by boosting your natural immune system. Herbalists prescribe six fresh cloves a day during serious cold and flu symptoms (eat parsley to neutralise the smell) or pop the pills instead. Oh, and garlic is also reported to slow down the ageing process. Cheaper than a pot of anti-wrinkle cream.

chapter 3

Toxin shock

41 **OK, so apart from the risks of heart and lung cancer, here's what else smoking can do to you:**

- *Cancer of the mouth and throat are more common in smokers (for obvious reasons), and so is cancer of the bladder, thanks to chemicals travelling through the body.*
- *Smoking exposes your body to the same degree of radiation as having 300 chest X-rays a year.*
- *Lung infections are common, and many smokers suffer from a persistent cough due to the overproduction of phlegm.*
- *Smoking ages the skin as it depletes the levels of vitamin C and damages the tissues that keep skin tight. Most long-term smokers look up to 10 years older than their actual age. Eyes will be more lined thanks to squinting, and sucking on a cigarette makes for deeper grooves around the mouth.*

Giving up is just about the best present you can give yourself. The effects of smoking touch every part of your body, but stop and all risks are reduced dramatically. Millions of people have stopped successfully, and three-quarters of them say it wasn't as difficult as they thought. But you must really want to give up or you'll be back puffing in no time. If you can't go it alone, join a support group or do it with a friend. But just do it.

42 **So-called convenience foods are anything but.** They are full of fat and sugar, not to mention a startling amount of preservatives and additives (check out those E numbers). The only thing you can be sure they don't contain is many nutrients. Walk on by on the way to the fresh food counter.

43 Ditch your salt cellar. Salt is essential to help regulate your body's fluid balance, but most of the food we eat already contains enough sodium for survival. And a high sodium intake also means potassium levels drop, leaving you feeling drowsy. Stop seasoning with salt and it won't take your taste buds long to get used to eating less (and tasting much more).

44 **If you live in a busy city, experts believe the air you breathe contains a risk similar to smoking 10 cigarettes a day.** When moving is not an option, fight pollution by filling up on foods containing antioxidant vitamins A, C and E (ie most fruit and veg) which help protect your body, or take an antioxidant vitamin supplement. And escape to the countryside occasionally to take big gulps of non-toxic air.

45 **Microwaves, televisions, telephones.** Twentieth-century toys contribute to toxic radiation, which can cause depression and much worse. Give yourself a break once in a while. Eat raw food, turn off your TV and take a relaxing bath instead, and don't spend your days with the phone glued to your ear.

46 **Beware negative ions emitted from your computer screen.** Sit at least 50cms away and give yourself (and your eyes) regular breaks.

47 **Drugs can save lives, but they also interfere with your body's biological defence system.** Don't ask for antibiotics unless you really need them as they can kill off good stuff as well as bad. Today's tough bacteria is more resistant which is why most doctors prescribe antibiotics less frequently. But if you have an infection that's acute or just won't go away, your doctor will know if you need a prescription.

48 **Your skin and hair hate chlorine as it strips away their natural protective oils,** causing dry, brittle hair and flaky, sore skin that also has a reduced resistance to UV damage. But swimming in a pool without chlorine would be even more harmful to your health as it's there to kill off bad bacteria in the water. Reverse the damage by always showering straight after your swim and washing hair to remove the chemicals.

TAKE ONE
A
DAY

49 **The air around you is alive with free radicals, all looking to attack and age your skin.** Protect from the outside as well as the inside by wearing a moisturiser containing antioxidants (look on the label) to mop up the mayhem.

50 Most illegal drugs are addictive, cause serious side effects (think mind and body) and can kill. Enough said?

51 Caffeine is a drug most of us take at least once a day, so what does it do?

- *Improves your mood*
- *Raises blood pressure*
- *Speeds up your heartbeat*
- *Makes you burn calories faster*
- *Gives you temporary energy.*

Nothing too bad, if drunk in moderation. But too much caffeine can also cause anxiety, high blood pressure and irregular breathing, and effects can last for up to seven hours. Limit yourself to four cups of coffee a day, and beware caffeine in other foods such as chocolate, canned drinks and cocoa – not such a good bedtime drink after all.

52 Alcohol is a sedative which slows down your thinking and movement, which is why moderate drinking (two drinks per day) is a stress reliever. But any more and we're talking fuzzy head, blurred vision, slurred speech and impaired judgement. And some-where not so far on is alcoholic poisoning, a severe toxic overload. Be sensible (if not always sober), and avoid alcohol completely during a detox time.

53 **A healthy body needs fat,**
just not as much as you'd like it to.
The right amount is no more than
30% of your total day's calorie
count, and only a third of this
should be saturated. What's the
difference? Red meat is mostly
saturated fat (and lots of it), and
so is the fat in butter and lard and
full-fat dairy products. The healthy
stuff can be found in fatty fish like
salmon and sardines, and olive oil.
Studies have also shown that our
weight has more to do with the
amount of saturated fats we eat
than the amount of calories. So
cut down on high fat foods and
you can expect better health –
and slimmer thighs.

54 Beware bacteria when washing up. Damp tea towels and washing-up tools are a breeding ground for bacteria. Change your cloths and brushes regularly, and let dishes dry naturally when possible. And wash dirty tea towels regularly instead of hanging up week-old ones to dry.

55 Exercising outdoors may be more pleasant than pumping away on a machine at the gym, but beware the air. Breathing in pollution will do nothing for your cardiovascular system, so wear a mask over your mouth when cycling, and get off busy roads and jog towards your local park instead. Grass is kinder than tarmac on joints too.

56 Farming methods have changed over the last few decades. Now the food you eat may have been sprayed with pesticides, chemical fertilisers and other toxic pollutants used in factory farming. Animals are also fed with processed foods, antibiotics and growth hormones before being slaughtered for your supper. The only way to be sure you're not chewing on a mouthful of chemicals? Buy organic.

57 **Sugar is a quick-fix energy food, but it also heaps on the calories.** Natural sugars can be found in fruit and vegetables, but we bet you get most of your sugar intake from other sweet and processed foods. Check ingredient labels for hidden sugar (also called fructose, glucose, maltose and syrup), and if one of these bad boys appears high on the list, you can be sure you're tucking into a fattening food. And not only does sugar contain few nutrients, it actually needs some (from your more healthy meals) to metabolise it.

58 **A polluted mind can be as bad for your body as a polluted environment.** Stress does many nasty things to your body including filling it up with adrenaline, which then floods the cells and breaks down your defences. When your head's stressed, your body has to deal with the toxic fall-out, and too much, too often can cause serious physical problems such as high blood pressure, diabetes and panic attacks. Identify the stresser and sort it out before it grinds you down.

59 **Negative thoughts are toxic.** Play mind games and turn a bad day into a good one. Train stuck in a tunnel? You've got an extra 10 minutes to read your book. Washing machine ate your jumper? You'll just have to go shopping for a new one. Use your head – don't lose it.

60 **Release your rage and rescue your body from an adrenaline overload.** The next time you stub your toe, scream the house down. Had a hard day at the office? Take a kickboxing class or go home and pummel your pillow.

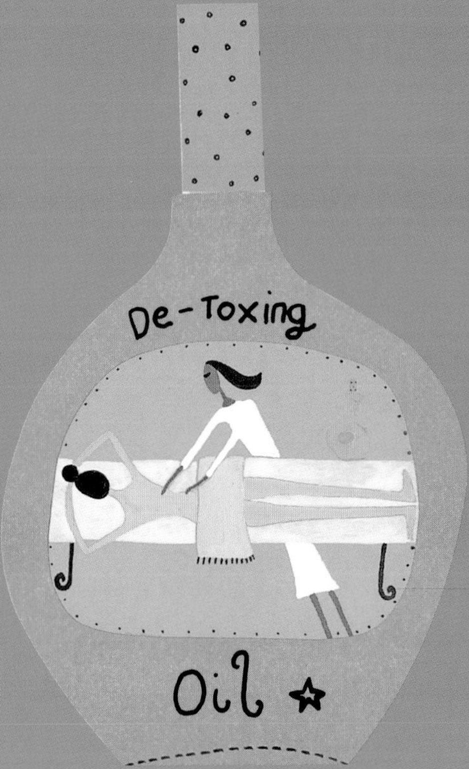
De-Toxing
Oil

chapter 4

Spa secrets

61 **Health spas may be the place to go to escape 21st-century stress,** but they've been around since 1700 when the Belgian town of Spa was a fashionable resort to relax in. Nowadays, what you get depends very much on where you go. Some spas concentrate on detoxing your body with serious fasting, while others offer a four-course meal along with lots of pampering. There's no substitute for a few days of the real thing – fresh air, peace and quiet, luxury and experts on hand – but that doesn't mean you can't DIY at home for a fraction of the cost. All you need is a couple of hours to spare, a handful of products and a lock on your bathroom door.

PALM BEACH
SPA

62 To stimulate digestion and soothe a bloated stomach, lie down and smooth either peppermint, parsley or mandarin essential oil over your abdomen. Work in big circles moving in a clockwise direction (the direction of your colon) and finish by gently kneading your fleshly bits.

63 Mud works like a hoover on the skin, drawing out dirt and pollution so they can be washed down the plughole along with the muddy water. The colour of mud depends on its mineral content. White clay boosts circulation and lymphatic flow, Fuller's Earth is extra-cleansing (find both in your local health food shop). Lie back in your bath for 20 minutes and don't be put off by the dirty-looking water. It's doing you good.

64 **Experts swear by body brushing to stimulate circulation and remove dead skin cells and other debris.** Almost a third of the body's waste can be eliminated through your skin, so get rid and see your skin glow. Oh, and forget expensive anti-cellulite lotions and potions. Skin brushing is more effective at stoking up your system than any cellulite cream. Invest in a natural bristle body brush and use dry before your bath or shower. Start at the soles of your feet and move up your legs and hips, then begin again at your fingertips and head towards your shoulders and back, finishing at your neck (never brush your breasts or face). The first time you brush, go gently as your skin needs to get used to the sensation. Brush daily and you'll be amazed how much rubbish your skin gladly gives up.

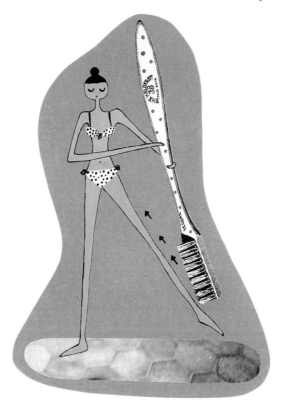

65 **If you're brave enough, start your day with a freezing cold shower** to wake you up and stimulate every part of your body. Much healthier than a double espresso. Cold water bathing also increases blood and lymph flow which speeds up the rate toxins leave your body, and boosts the production of white blood cells – your infection fighters. Stay under for 30 seconds to one minute before switching the dial back to warm.

66 **Can't face the full body experience?** Then paddle around in a bath of cold water for an instant immune booster.

67 Unblock your system with a salt bath. Add two cups of either sea salt or Epsom salts (from your local chemist) to warm water. Soak for 20 minutes and the heat will encourage toxins to leave through your open pores. Top up the hot tap to maintain the temperature and avoid using soap which will interfere with the salt's suction action. Only indulge in this once a month as it is a powerful detox treatment. Take a salt bath late at night and go to bed feeling relaxed and deep-down clean.

68 Another sweaty salt spa-type treatment. Add warm water to a cup of sea salt and massage the paste into your body. Use firm, circular movements over problem areas (think bottom, legs and upper arms) and avoid delicate skin. Rinse the mixture off in your shower and then rub yourself dry. Now hop into bed and cosy up. The more you sweat, the more the toxins are shifting. But keep a glass of water handy to replenish lost liquid through the night.

69 **Make your own detox wrap at home.** Blend together one cup of olive oil with one cup of grapefruit juice and two teaspoons of dried thyme. Massage the mixture onto your thighs, bottom and hips. Then wrap your body in cling film to create the all-important heat needed for your skin to soak in.

70 **For a detox treatment, add rosemary, cypress or lemon oil to your bath** as the heat will encourage your capillaries to come to the surface and absorb the oil straight into your bloodstream. Use no more than six drops and sprinkle in after your bath water has run so the vapours don't escape in the steam.

82

71 The ultimate detox, colonic irrigation claims to shift years of debris from your bowel. Practitioners claim the average meat eater's colon contains between 2–4kg of impacted waste. We say, perhaps nature intended it that way. Not surprisingly, customers either love or hate it. Most important is to find a reputable therapist, but if you're the least bit shy, perhaps you should pass this one by.

72 A little light facial massage can boost circulation and improve lymphatic drainage. Use your thumbs to apply pressure under your cheekbones and your index finger to gently pinch the flesh on the top.

73 Spas love seaweed as it stimulates the metabolism, encourages fat burning, flushes out toxins and boosts your immune system. The elements in seaweed pass straight through your skin to deep cleanse and detoxify. Soak in a shop-bought seaweed-based bath at home for no more than 20 minutes and then wrap yourself in a blanket and rest for another 15 minutes.

74 Spas say sea water is literally food for the skin as it contains essential minerals medically proven to promote health. These minerals are similar to those in the body's blood plasma, which makes them easily absorbed through your skin. Blasts of salty water are aimed at your thighs, hips and bottom to stimulate circulation and tone through elimination of toxins. But for a cheap substitute, take a trip to the seaside and let the waves of salty water wash your wobbles away.

75 **Use your power shower to stimulate blood circulation, improve skin tone and shift cellulite.** Move a high pressure shower head over legs and bottom in the direction of your heart, and alternate between sprays of hot and cold water for 30 seconds each. To brighten a tired, sluggish complexion, aim a not-so-powerful cold shower at your face, working in small circles, and pat dry.

76 Make your own seaweed sludge. You can buy fresh seaweed from the supermarket, or health food shops. Put a little at a time in your blender or food processor as it can be tough to cut up. Add two tablespoons of a skin-friendly oil (grapeseed and wheatgerm are good) and whiz away until you've got your paste. Apply it fresh to trouble spots such as legs, bottom and stomach and then wrap yourself in cling film for maximum absorption and minimum mess. Relax for 20 minutes and then jump in the shower and rinse yourself off.

77 Don't indulge in a serious seaweed treatment just before going to bed, as the powerful ingredients absorbed through your skin will keep you wide awake.

78 If you can't stomach seaweed, take kelp supplements instead. A pill a day is an easy way to protect your body from pollution, boost your circulation and maintain a stable metabolic rate.

79 **Heat can deep-cleanse and detox by encouraging your body to sweat away water and toxins.** Check if your gym or leisure centre has a sauna or steam room and pop in after your activity to eliminate impurities through your pores. But stay no longer than 10 minutes in any heated room, and avoid using a sauna or steam room as a hangover cure (the high temperature will dehydrate you even more). Speed up a sauna detox by using essential oils in the water you pour over hot coals. Add five to six drops of cypress oil to one ladle of water, and don't sprinkle oil straight onto the coals as it'll spit back at you.

80 **After any detox treatment, wrap up warm and relax with a cup of cleansing herbal tea.** Ingredients to look out for include dandelion, nettle, burdock, lemon and ginger.

chapter 5

Detox your life

81 Life depends on plants.

All environmental conditions are reliant on plants taking up water and releasing it through their leaves (if a rain forest is cut down, the area will soon become a desert). Plants are also responsible for the oxygen level in the atmosphere as they suck in carbon dioxide and release oxygen back into the air. Plant filled spaces are instantly relaxing. They increase the oxygen content of the air, improve humidity, and house plants such as Goosefoot, Peace Lilies and Peperomia have been found to cleanse many pollutants from the air.

82 Plants can benefit your work environment too.

They put moisture back into air-conditioned offices, and some plants have been found to absorb soundwaves, creating a more peaceful workplace.

83 Life too noisy?

Then spend a day in silence. Read, write and empty your head of worries. Tomorrow's another day and you can start it with a clear head.

84 **Do mobile phones fry your brain?** Compensation claims made by heavy users who developed brain tumours remain controversial. But play safe by using yours as little as possible (think of the bill) and keep the antenna well away from your head.

85 **Computers cause a build-up of static electricity which attracts irritating dust particles to the air around you.** Cut down on static by wearing natural fibres, which are poor conductors of electricity, and fit your computer with an anti-static screen.

86 **You probably spend more time sitting at your desk than anywhere else,** so you may as well make it a better place to be. A cluttered desk makes for a cluttered mind, so clear away anything you don't use at least once a week.

Bin.

87 Why have friends who bring you down? Negative people drain your energy, so clear them out of your life and make space for the positive ones who make you happy.

88 Detox your mind and you'll see things more clearly.

- *What don't you like about your life?* Write down ways to change it for the better. Whether that just means eating more healthily or long-term changes such as studying, anything that makes you feel better is a good thing. Boredom is exhausting.

- *What makes you stressed?* Everyone has their weak spot. Identify yours and you'll be halfway to lightening the load.

- *Need a confidence boost?* Write down all your personality plus points, all the things you're good at and all the things you've done well.

- *Face down your demons.* Apologise for things you've done in the past you still feel rotten about. Even if you write a letter and never send it, it'll help banish those bad feelings.

89 **Spring clean your home with natural eco-friendly products that won't add extra chemicals and toxins to the atmosphere.** And don't skip any awkward bits. Pull out all the furniture and vacuum every nook and cranny. That hidden rubbish is filling your room with stagnant energy. Get rid and feel the positive flow.

90 **The ancient Chinese art of feng shui aims to adjust your surroundings for a more successful life.** The idea is to clear out clutter and boost the flow of chi energy through your home (just like shiatsu and acupuncture do in your body). Feng shui practitioners believe a building can be divided into eight wedges (like a cake), and each area has a different flow of energy which can affect your own.

- *The east section is influenced by the rising sun and associated with ambition.*
- *The southeast feels the sun as it rises and makes you feel more creative.*
- *The south is the warmest part of your home and also the most passionate.*
- *The southwest sees the sun as it starts to fall and makes you feel more practical.*
- *The west section faces the sunset and is associated with contentment and romance.*
- *The northwest is influenced by the end of the day and a sense of control.*

- *The north relates to the middle of the night and inner peace.*
- *The northeast feels cold and encourages you to be more motivated.*

Spend time in these specific areas of your home and feel the charge of chi energy.

ECO CLEAN!

91 **Detox your wardrobe.**
Clothes you never wear just
take up room. And stop fooling
yourself. You're never going to fit
into those size 10 jeans again.
But don't dump everything. Take
all your rejects to the local charity
shop. They'll be very grateful.

92 **Make a place for everything**
and then you won't waste precious time and energy searching
for door keys, bills, letters, and
so on.

93 **Clean your windows
regularly.** You want the sun to
shine through and light up your
home, not be blocked by layers
of dirt and dust.

94 Clearing out clutter is therapeutic. Getting rid of items you keep 'just in case' will re-energise your home and head. If you're still reluctant, bag up anything you haven't used for six months and put it in the garden shed. Then in another six months, if you haven't missed a thing, give the bag to charity, or have a car boot sale and make some money from your newfound tidiness.

95 Detox your bathroom. If it's full of year-old bottles, save space (and time in the morning) by throwing out what you don't use every week. And ditch the guilt. If that expensive cream brought you out in a rash, you're never going to use it no matter how much it cost. You may also be surprised how much is lurking in the back of your cabinet that's well past its sell-by-date.

Time to throw out:
- *Mascara* – three months
- *Foundation* – six months
- *Lipstick and powder* – one year
- *Eye cream* – one year
- *Moisturiser* – two years
- *Sunscreens* have a shelf-life of 30 months, but to be on the safe side, bin your half used bottles every year, as baking on the beach will lower their SPF power dramatically.

96 Your car is a small home of its own. Clear out the empty cartons on the floor, dog hairs on the seats and sweet wrappers in the ashtray. You'll feel better every time you open the door.

97 De-junk a make-up bag bursting with cosmetics. Be honest. You only ever wear two lipsticks anyway. If you can't bear to throw the rest out, leave them where you might need them (car, desk drawer, handbag etc). And give your make-up tools a clean too. Every day you wipe them over your face and then put them back (often damp) in your bag. Wash your sponges and brushes with a little shampoo and warm water to get rid of budding germs.

98 Unfinished business zaps your energy, so get up to date.
Pay bills on time, return phone calls immediately and fill in tedious forms the minute they drop on the mat. That way you can live in the present with nothing hanging over your head.

99 Exercise is essential for detoxing your body. It fills your lungs with energy-boosting oxygen, encourages your lymphatic system to shed waste, and makes you feel fantastic. If you're fasting, a gentle walk is enough to keep your insides ticking along. But at other times, 30–40 minutes of aerobic exercise is what's needed to gain bumper benefits. Aerobic means anything that gets your heart beating faster and your breathing deeper. Brisk walking, swimming, jogging, cycling or even skipping all count as a serious workout (with no leotard required).

100 **Sometimes you need a totally new perspective on life.** If you've recently ended a relationship, left a job or just feel deflated, think about foreign travel. Seeing new places and meeting new people will change your mindset, and all those things that seemed so important back home will suddenly lose their power over you.